One More Time

One More Time

by
Gil Stevenson

DORRANCE PUBLISHING CO., INC.
PITTSBURGH, PENNSYLVANIA 15222

Copyright © 1992 by Gil Stevenson
All Rights Reserved
ISBN # 0-8059-3260-7
Printed in the United States of America

First Printing

TABLE OF CONTENTS

Preface vii

"THE MONORAIL" AND OTHER STORIES
Tiger Stripes and Reporting Marks 3
Petie and the Woof 5
I Was a Pig Farmer in Gadara 6
The Monorail 7
Lissomei 9

FROM A DEVIL'S ADVOCATE'S NOTEBOOK
Curiosity, Love, and Dominion 19
Sociological Note 20
Historical Note 20
Awards 21
Running Away 21
Thoughts 22
The Spirit of 76 22
Fraternal Note 22
"A Thousand Points of Light" 23
Fiscal Note 23
The Bloods and the Crips .23
Patriotic Note 24
How to Feed A Husband 24
Archaeological Note 25
Economic Note 25
Freedom Fighters 25
A Beleaguered Minority 26
Make War, Not Love 26

A Hundred Portraits 27
No Nukes = No War? 28
Treadmill Musings 28
Pro-choice *is* Pro-life 29
Buy American 30
Security 30
Wisdom 31
Political Note 31
Exegetical Note 31
Ethnic Note 32
Zoological Note 32

MY SMALL AND GENTLE ONES
The Wildlife Connection 35
So Many Pussies 36
A Thought 36
Symbiosis 37
Pasture-walking 37
For Poki 38
Cat Song 39
February Thaw 39
First Walk 40

THE LANGUAGE WE SPEAK
How Close Do We Come? 43
Stylistic Note 43
Transformational Grammar 44
What is a Language? 46
"In...of" vs "In the..of" 47
"Much," "Very," and "Very Much" 49
Does English Have an Ethical Dative? 52
New Suffixes 53
An 'Agentive-Possessive'? 54

DOMESTIC VERSES
The Macintosh Blues 57
Furzle-Bushes 58
Dumpster Song 59
Fantasy 60
Security 60

A Valentine	.61
Valentine Song	.61
January Song	.62
19th Anniversary	.62
Being	.63
Anniversary	.63
Treadmill	.64
Presence	.64
24th Anniversary	.65
Spouse	.65
Bird Song	.66
25th Anniversary	.66
Equinox	.67
Silver Anniversary	.67
A Valentine for Felicia	.68
Sandy, Home for a Visit	.68
Next Visit	.69
A Day in August	.69
For Carol and Summer (II)	.70
November Song	.71
A Ballad for May 23rd	.72
To Wyoming	.73
Winter Walk	.74
Lilac Time	.75
The Ballad of Nutter's Lawn	.76
Almost Home	.77
For Wendy and Wanda	.77
A Guest at Our Table	.78

PREFACE

Creative people, whether painters, woodworkers, or cooks, often like to use their own creations as gifts. Every Christmas for twenty-five years I have done this with my writings, in the form of a booklet of my latest creations for family and friends. The contents of these, plus other material, have later gone into a series of hardcover books published by Dorrance & Co. Herein is what I have written since the publication of *7000 Feet Closer To Heaven* in 1984.

Since most of the cat pieces were written several years ago, I regret to say that most of the cats they were about are no longer around. Life at The Acres goes on, children grow up and move away into lives of their own, and the feline population fluctuates. We cherish them while they are with us, give them the best care we can, and remember them fondly.

The Acres
Howell, Wyoming
June 1991

"THE MONORAIL" AND OTHER STORIES

TIGER STRIPES AND REPORTING MARKS

A little old lady in Howell, Wyoming (which as you all know, is the center of the universe) kept a large tiger as a pet. He was a sweet old thing and he loved people, so when anyone came to see the little old lady, the tiger would go up to the visitor and purr. Unfortunately a large tiger, even a sweet one, has a pretty formidable purr and the visitor would think he was growling and flee.

Now the little old lady felt sad about not having any company because of her pet, so she decided to leap on her little old bike and tool down to the hardware store for a bucket of tiger paint. She figured, if she could paint out the tiger's stripes so he wouldn't *look* like a tiger, her guests wouldn't run away when he purred. So she did, and he didn't—but would it work?

Well, the very next day the little old lady's stockbroker came out to Howell to urge her to buy Hoist and Derrick stock because the Federal Reserve was going to need lots of hoists and derricks to pick up the economy. To be sure, the tiger didn't look like a tiger anymore but his purr was as formidable as ever, so the stockbroker didn't sell any Hoist and Derrick stock; he just, rather hastily, left. When he got back to town he went to see his friend who ran the cat house at the zoo and told his experience: "I was all set to make my pitch when the biggest mountain lion I ever saw came out and growled at me."

Said the zookeeper, "I think I'd better go out and have a look."

Meanwhile the little old lady washed the tiger paint off her pet. Concealing his stripes obviously hadn't done any good, so he might as well look like himself. When the zookeeper arrived, the tiger, stripes and all, went out to meet him and purred—but the zookeeper didn't run away. He knew a big, sweet old tiger when he saw one, so he ran up to the tiger, gave him a big hug and rubbed him behind his ears, so the tiger purred louder than ever.

But what was the little old lady's husband doing all this time? Well, he was at a meeting of the board of directors of a fine old American railroad that was going broke and the directors were trying to figure out what to do. One of them suggested asking the ICC for permission to merge with one of their more prosperous neighbors, but another pointed out that the ICC would take too long to make up its mind and they didn't have that kind of time.

Finally the little old lady's husband spoke up: "Why not try magic? We've tried everything else. We'll change our reporting marks* and paint everything blue."

"But that would confuse people," another director protested. "They wouldn't know we were us." The little old lady's husband just grinned (a little wickedly, I fear). Nobody had a better idea, so magic it was. They changed their reporting marks and painted everything blue, and, do you know what? The railroad went broke anyway.

Now these would be pretty dumb stories if they didn't have a moral to them. Can you guess what it is? You hate guessing games too? Okay, I'll tell you:

You may as well be yourself.

---

* The code initials on a freight car that tell railroad people who it belongs to.

PETIE AND THE WOOF

Once there was a little girl named Petie who had a pet woof that went wherever Petie went. The woof liked to chase jackalopes but he never caught one and wouldn't have known what to do with it if he had. "Why do you chase jackalopes?" Petie asked him one day. "Don't you know there is no such animal?" This didn't bother the woof; for him the chase was the thing. (When Petie grew up, she would learn that people were the same way: what counted was the *pursuit* of happiness, whether or not there really was such an animal.)

One day Petie and her folks and, of course, the woof, were picnicking in the nearby woods when the woof spied a jackalope, so off he went. Nobody worried about this because he always gave up eventually and came back to the picnic grounds, or sometimes he would be waiting for them at home. This time, however, was different. Somehow he got turned around, and the harder he tried to get back the more lost he became. Tired, hungry, and bedraggled, he plodded on through fields and forests until he came to a village. Here he went up to a little boy in the street and told him, "I'm hungry and lost. I am a weary woof!" The little boy ran home and shouted, "Mommy! Mommy! There's a shaggy beast in the red light district that says he's a werewolf!"

"You naughty boy! What were you doing in the red light district? *A WHAT? A WEREWOLF?*"

The alarm spread and the tocsin sounded, and sounded, and sounded until it woke up the mayor, who told his henchman to turn on the anti-tocsin and stop that infernal racket. By then the streets were deserted and all the good people of the village, and some of the other people too, were hiding safely in their root cellars and bomb shelters and hall closets.

The weary woof plodded on until he got to the exurbs. Here he went up to the house of a little old lady who lived with her pet tiger and her husband the retired railroad director. (Actually, it was the railroad that retired. When it went belly-up, the director had nothing left to direct.) Now, the tiger was a sweet old thing and as gentle as a kitten, but he had such a powerful purr that siding salesmen and tax assessors treated the old couple with the utmost respect. As for werewolves, when he was young and fierce, he used to eat them for breakfast and they still treated him with respect if only for old time's sake.

"Martha, there's a beast at the door that claims he's a werewolf. Would you please come and check it out?" said the little old lady's husband. She came to the door and looked the bedraggled woof over.

"You don't look like a werewolf to me. You look like a plain old dorg," she told him.

"Well, I am," the woof replied, "but my mistress says I'm a woof."

"How old is your mistress?"

"She's six years old," replied the woof.

"That figures," said the little old lady, who had grandchildren of her own. "I think we'd better get you something to eat."

Now, they had plenty of dorg food in the house because that's what the tiger ate when the supermarket was out of tiger food, so the weary woof dined well, and after a bath and a brush he didn't look like a weary woof anymore, but more like a plain old dorg. Eventually, of course, he did get home to Petie and he still chased jackalopes, but never again, no matter how tired he got, did he tell anybody that he was a weary woof.

The Gospels tell us what happened to the famous Gardarene swine, but what happened to the farmer? Here, in his own words, is his story.

I WAS A PIG FARMER IN GADARA

My people don't eat pork, so how did a good Galilean Jew come to raise pigs? Well, we're part of the Roman Empire now, and I don't think even the Maccabees could change that; and the Roman soldiers like pork. My neighbors don't think it's very patriotic of me to keep the Roman army in pig meat, but I figure these people are here to exploit us, so why not exploit them a little? Why not make a buck off these guys?

I was making a real good living, too. I had a beautiful wife, 2.17 adorable children, a lovely home, and a late model donkey cart in the driveway and a late model donkey to move it. Man, I had it *made*. Then one day this crazy preacher from across the lake came over and spooked my pigs so they all ran off a cliff and drowned in the lake. That wiped me *out*, man. The insurance company wouldn't pay for the pigs because the policy didn't cover miracles. The loan sharks in the temple foreclosed on my house, the dealer repossessed the donkey and the cart too, and my wife ran off with a feed salesman and took the kids with her.

And that preacher didn't say so much as, "Sorry about that." He just looked into my soul and said, "Follow me," so here I am. I was flat-broke, man. What else could I do?

THE MONORAIL

After he registered for the meeting and checked out his quarters, he looked over the program. Seeing that none of the papers he wanted to hear would be read until the next day, he decided to while away this summer afternoon in Seattle. He hailed a cab and asked the driver to take him downtown, on the way asking him if the monorail out to the exposition park was still running. The diver assured him it was and offered to drop him off at the nearest station.

"No, I want the whole trip. Take me to where it starts, please." For a bigger fare the cabbie was happy to oblige. Limping slightly as he left the cab, he climbed the stairs to the elevated platform and entered the fast-filling first monorail car. To his surprise, a slim, brown-haired woman followed him and sat down beside him. Seeing her hazel eyes and the slightly angular lines of her friendly, intelligent face, he thought of someone he knew a long time ago, but for this to be her was too much of a long shot. Not until the doors closed and the train began to move did either of them speak.

"Excuse me," she said, "please don't think I'm crazy, but is your name Steve?"

"Well, yes," was his somewhat startled reply, and then, "You must be Ellen, the girl who gave me a guided tour of the park and showed me where you worked?"

"The wonderful man who held my hand as we jumped over a puddle and went skipping down the path to my booth like a couple of kids?"

"The lovely girl who sold me some trinkets for my sister's kids and seemed relieved to learn I was single, though she declined my invitation to dinner because her boyfriend was meeting her after work?"

"The same," Ellen replied, "and when you left you gave me a beautiful smile and told me something odd and rather lovely." (Was this really him? She had to make sure!) "Do you remember what it was?"

He remembered that moment ten years ago as if it was this morning. "I said, 'Good-bye, Ellen. Have a good life'!"

"Oh, and I have!" She was really excited now. Then, reminiscing, "Poor Mark. We had a nice date that night, but all I could think of was skipping down the path with a total stranger named Steve. But Mark and I did get married. He was a good guy and we had a nice life, but he was in the Air Force. He was killed in Viet Nam."

"Oh, Ellen! I'm sorry!" Steve paused for a moment, then added gently, "I was there too. In the Navy."

"Is that how your leg got hurt? I noticed you were limping a little when we got on the train."

"I'm afraid it's only on television that the bad guys are always such lousy shots. Would you believe a sailor getting shot in the leg by a sniper?"

"Mark told me it wasn't a very orthodox war."

"I wish I'd known him," Steve said, then, seeing the consternation about his leg clouding her lovely face, he added reassuringly, "Cheer up. The VA's wooden legs are the best in the West. I can still skip."

"What brings you to Seattle this time, Steve?"

"I'm here for a meeting of the Linguistic Society. I teach the stuff at Euphoria College in the great State of Kebansas. And you?"

"I'm a research professor of microbiology at the University here; and I have two children: Mark, who wants to be a flier like his father; and Stephanie, who wants to be a microbiologist even though she's a little vague about what one does."

"Stephanie? For the princess of Monaco?"

"No, silly. Mark never knew this, but I named her for you."

"You named your daughter after a guy you only knew for a couple of hours?"

Ellen changed the subject. "What made you take the monorail today?"

"Just an impulse," he answered. "How about you?"

"Just an impulse," said Ellen. They were silent, awed by the workings of fate, as the train hummed along its single overhead rail and Seattle glided by beneath its big windows.

"Steve, did you ever marry?" Ellen wasn't sure if this was a proper thing to ask, but she had to know.

"No, I never did. I was busy working on my degree and then I got caught up in the war...and I kept thinking of a girl I knew in Seattle."

"Me?" she asked shyly.

"You."

She noticed for the first time his strong sun-browned hand enfolding her graceful but capable one. "How long have we been holding hands?" she wondered.

"About ten years, I think." Though Ellen had her romantic side, she was basically a practical girl and this, coming from a man she hadn't seen for ten years, struck her as a bit metaphysical; yet somehow she liked it.

Ellen got her courage up and asked him, "Do you believe in love at first sight?"

"I do now. I think that must be what happened to us, but we didn't realize it."

"It's happening again, isn't it?"

"I still want you to have a good life, but I won't say good-bye. Ellen, will you marry me?"

He was sure he saw her eyes twinkle as she replied, "Only if you hold my hand when we get to the puddles."

"Of course. *Now* will you have dinner with me?"

Swiftly, smoothly, the train eased into its last station. With a soft pneumatic hiss the doors slid open and the car was quickly emptied of all but two of its passengers. With a broad smile, the conductor admonished the two that were left:

"Everybody out, folks. This is the end of the line."

"No, it isn't," Steve smiled back as he and Ellen skipped hand in hand out onto the platform, "it's only the beginning."

LISSOMEI

Ellen Fremedon, a young widow with two small children, was a microbiologist in Seattle when she married Steve Lutchka, a Viet Nam veteran who taught linguistics at Euphoria in the prairie state of Kebansas. Now, the better part of a decade later, while Mark and Stephanie entered their teens, Ellen was still a microbiologist in Seattle while Steve taught linguistics at Euphoria. Thanks to this arrangement, every Christmas vacation, spring break, summer recess, or holiday weekend that they could be together, whether in Washington or Kebansas, was like another honeymoon.

"Absence really does make the heart grow fonder," Ellen once said, to which Steve added gallantly, "So does your presence."

Once more, school was out for the summer and they were all at Steve's house on the bank of the Kebansas River, which was so broad and tranquil at Euphoria as to be frequently taken for a lake. Upon her arrival, Ellen was pleased to note that Steve's small sloop was still moored at the dock in front of his house. A few days later, on a June morning perfect for sailing, they were on their way across the river to visit Sanggarius and Mozzarella Morgan in South Prairie. (They had invited the kids to come along but they declined politely, pleading a new Grateful Dead album that they were anxious to hear. With the house to themselves, they could turn the volume up to the ear-shattering level that young people seemed to prefer.) Ellen had been racing sailboats on Lake Washington since she was twelve years old and she took her sailing seriously, so Steve knew she was itching to get her hands on the tiller and make this craft really go. Steve had been in the Navy long enough to respect good seamanship, so he wasn't sure which he enjoyed more: sailing the little sloop himself, or watching Ellen handle it.

She adjusted the mainsail to suit the soft downstream breeze that was lightly rippling the placid water of the Kebansas, then busied herself with setting the jib exactly right. "My dad told me that to win races you have to make sure the jib does its fair share of the work. I don't know how many frustrated mariners I have seen fiddling endlessly with the mainsail and neglecting the jib," Ellen explained.

"I know," Steve sympathized, "I've seen Sanggarius do that."

"Smart-ass!" said his spouse, "Gus's boat doesn't have a jib."

Sanggarius Morgan was a successful novelist and historian whom the critics were fond of comparing to James A Michener. His wife taught zoology at South Prairie University. "What romantic names Gus and Rella have," remarked Ellen as they neared the Morgans' dock, "like Romeo and Juliet."

"Or Lutchka and Fremedon?" Steve suggested.

Soon Steve and Sanggarius were comfortably nursing tall drinks on the Morgans' wide porch, shaded by grand old cottonwoods and looking out over the river, while Ellen and Mozzarella settled in the kitchen to make snacks and discuss the ethics of genetic engineering.

"How did you come to get so interested in history?" Steve's friend asked him.

"As a linguist I have to be, Gus. You can't study languages in a vacuum, though some of my colleagues may seem to. Language is a human activity, something that people *do*, and the story of a language is largely the story of the people who speak it. There is an English language because people speak English, and its history is the history of those people."

"Did you know that South Prairie almost seceded from the Union during the Civil War?" Gus said when it was his turn, "Not to join the Confederacy, but to join Canada. Most of our western states were settled from the east, but South Prairie was mainly settled from the north. Most of our first people came down from Canada. They were afraid they would be dragged into a war that didn't concern them. Slavery was on its last legs anyway, so why fight a war over it? And why shouldn't the Southerners have their own country if that's what they wanted?"

"No wonder South Prairie is called the Copperhead State," said Steve, again surprising his friend by his knowledge of history. "So what did the South really want?"

"Southerners who abhorred slavery, and there were more of them than most histories let on, fought as hard for the South as anyone else. They wanted what we fought for in the Revolution: control of their own economy, and the right to run their own show. They were convinced that they would be better off economically if they were a country of their own. Question: Was preserving the Union really worth all that bloodshed and bitterness?"

"Apparently the people of South Prairie thought not," Steve said. "So what happened?"

"They actually went so far as to change our official name to the Province of South Prairie in anticipation of their union with Canada, and you know what? I have never been able to find any record of the name having been changed back. We are still the Province of South Prairie!"

"That means we have forty-five states, plus four commonwealths and a province. But what happened to the union with Canada?" Steve wondered.

"Canada didn't want us," said Gus.

"Gus, you mix a mean whitlock," Steve said as he and Ellen, with their hosts, strolled back down to the dock to get ready for the trip home, "but Ellen will get us home safely. Just between you and me, she's a better sailor that I am anyway."

Sanggarius chuckled. "Better not let the Navy hear you say that."

With the downstream breeze freshening and the designated sailor in charge, they were soon halfway back to Kebansas. With the world to themselves and Steve in a mellow mood, Ellen seemed to decide that this was a propitious time to come out with her news: "Lissomei is back in the States. She may be coming to see us one of these days."

"Which Lissomei?" Steve teased her.

"You old woolly wolf! How many Lissomeis do you know?"

At least three: Lissomei Baldwin, Lissomei Rexingdon, and Lissomei Ferguson," Steve rattled off the maiden name and both married names of the one and only Lissomei that anyone in Kebansas ever heard of.

Lissomei was a South African girl whom Ellen had known since her college days. Steve had met her a few times and liked her well enough, so he was mildly puzzled as to why Ellen had waited to break what did not strike him as especially grave news. He was soon to find out.

As they eased into the dock they heard music coming from the house, something not in itself unusual with Mark and Stephanie around, but as they listened more closely to a lively tune on a guitar, and a lilting contralto singing it, Ellen said, "That doesn't sound like the Grateful Dead to me."

Steve listened to the words. "That sounds like Afrikaans."

"How can you tell?"

"You married a linguist, my love. Remember?"

"Afrikaans?"

"Lissomei!" they both shouted at once, and ran up the path to the house. Seated cross-legged on the living room floor, with her back against the sofa, was a small, sprightly woman picking out a spirited melody on Steve's big guitar and singing in her native tongue to a pair of enchanted teenagers.

After the first round of excited exclamations and hugs, Ellen scolded her fondly, "Why didn't you let us know you were coming?" Lissomei looked at the kids.

"We knew Aunt Liss was coming," Mark confessed, "but she made us promise not to tell. She wanted it to be a surprise."

"That it was," Steve affirmed.

Ellen was curious. "And if you did tell?"

"And spoil Aunt Liss's surprise?" Stephanie explained solemnly. "She wouldn't sing for us again. Ever!"

Ellen smiled. "That does sound pretty dire," she agreed.

After the kids had retired to their own domain to listen to the Grateful Dead, and Lissomei had gone up to the guest room to get settled in, Steve asked his wife, "Why would two normal American teenagers be totally spellbound by a woman singing children's songs in Afrikaans?"

"Who knows?" Ellen replied, not too helpfully, "but I think those two would be spellbound by Lissomei whatever she did."

A couple of days later, Ellen and the kids went shopping in Euphoria, leaving Steve to entertain their guest. "Why don't you sail over to South Prairie and introduce Lissomei to the Morgans?" Ellen had suggested. "She's a good sailor. She can help you with the boat."

Lissomei was comparing her own unusual name to Mozzarella's. "It's a family name. One of my ancestors was an Irish lass named Melissa O'May who emigrated to the Transvaal at the time of the Boer wars." Her Boer friends shortened it to Liss O'May and spelled it the Afrikaans way."

Later, Sanggarius was asking her, "How much longer do you think apartheid will last?"

Lissomei replied, "Slavery did not end in the United States because the North won the Civil War. It ended because it was obsolete. It was no longer acceptable in a civilized modern nation. Our complicated and clumsy system of racial segregation will end the same way, probably not all at once, but gradually phased out.

"You must remember," she continued, "that we have been in our country as long as you've been in yours, and we haven't treated the native population any worse than you have treated the Indians. Now suppose that your Navaho reservation was an independent, sovereign nation whose people lived according to their own customs, chose their own government, and flew their own flag. We have four such nations, carved out of South African territory: Bophuthatswana, Ciskei, Transkei, and Venda. They provide an alternative to apartheid for at least some of our aborigines.

"If the U.S. really wants to help, it should recognize these nations and help them get on their feet, instead of imposing sanctions on South Africa, which only hurt innocent people. Our native people wouldn't have to put up with apartheid if their own little countries were thriving.

"By the way, Gus, I was happy to hear you pronounce 'apartheid' right."

Steve added, "A lot of people call it 'apart-hide' as if it was a German word. Afrikaans is Germanic, but it's certainly not German. The 'ei' in Afrikaans is pronounced like the 'ei' in 'their'."

"How about that, Lissomei?" said Gus. "Linguistics is really good for something after all. Right now it's whitlock-drinking time on the prairie."

There were other occasions when Steve and Lissomei had each other to themselves: a picnic at Riverview Park, a tour of the Euphoria campus, a sailing excursion up the river. Since Ellen had a busy schedule, and Lissomei had arrived unexpectedly, they saw nothing strange about this, though after a while Steve was beginning to wonder a little.

One evening Steve and Ellen had been watching television and were still sitting together on the living room sofa, holding hands as they often still did. Stephanie, Mark, and Lissomei were down on the dock waiting to watch the moon rise over the river. "Do you remember your marriage vows, Steve?" Ellen asked unexpectedly.

"I promised to hold your hand when we got to the puddles," he replied.

"That's the one," she said, giving his hand an extra squeeze. "Tell me, are you falling in love with Lissomei?"

"Of course. Anyone who wouldn't be has no soul."

"I'm glad to know I have a soul, darling, because I love her too."

"I seem to recall that you were roommates at graduate school."

"More than just roommates, honey. Much more!"

"Are you telling me I have a bisexual wife?"

"I guess I am."

Steve was silent for a while, digesting this news. Finally Ellen asked him, gently, "How do you feel?"

"I wish I knew. I don't even know how I'm *supposed* to feel. Sort of diminished, I guess, like I've just discovered that I'm not everything to you that I thought I was. What did Mark think of this?" Mark had been Ellen's first husband, a fighter pilot killed in Viet Nam.

"He didn't know Liss and I were lovers. Either she was back in Africa or he was in Viet Nam. They never met."

"Don't you think I should have known about this sooner?" Steve protested.

"I wanted you to know, but I wanted you to get to know Lissomei first."

"You figured that I could live with your loving Lissomei if I loved her myself?"

"Something like that."

"Well, I guess it worked. God knows there's little enough love in the world. It should never be wrong to love someone."

"Yes, my darling. Let's go watch the moon come up."

Hand in hand they strolled down to the dock.

NOTES TO "LISSOMEI"

"Lissomei" (pronounced LISS-o-may) is a sequel to "The Monorail." The story itself, and the characters in it, are purely fictitious, as are the states of Kebansas and South Prairie and the river that separates them.

The whitlock, however, is a real drink, created by the author during the 1960s and named for his boss.

Afrikaans, decended from 17th century Dutch, is one of the two official languages of South Africa. Bophuthatswana, Ciskei, Transkei, and Venda are real nations.

FROM A DEVIL'S ADVOCATE'S NOTEBOOK

CURIOSITY, LOVE, AND DOMINION

Living things are never permanent. They perpetuate their kind, but not themselves. Species last, individuals do not. It is our very mortality that makes evolution possible: a few thousand more tries, and maybe the species can do better! With each new generation it gets another chance.

Most forms of life are kept busy just keeping themselves going and propagating the species. Humans are almost unique in having enough leisure to devote themselves to other pursuits. What motivations do we have for these other pursuits? What forces impel us to do what we do once the basic needs of survival and procreation are met?

One of them is surely curiosity; the hankering to find out what lies beyond the horizon or beyond our solar system, the urge to see what things consist of and how they work, from our own bodies to the Milky Way, from the core of the atom to the intellect of the dolphin. Without our insatiable curiosity would we have any science? Without science would we have any civilization?

Another of the great forces that motivate people is love. It motivated the construction of the Taj Mahal. It inspired the Christian religion. It gave us the great romances that make up so much of our literature, such as the story of Romeo and Juliet, that of Rhett Butler and Scarlett O'Hara, or even my own little story of The Monorail. It gave us Valentine's Day and our family's celebration of Maundy Thursday, and brought us all the way to Florida to visit our daughters, and our daughters all the way to Wyoming to visit us. Deeds both tragic and wonderful have been done for love. What would our world be without it?

The lust for power, for dominion over territory and people, has shaped human history more than anything else. It has been responsible for almost all of our wars. The great empire builders, from Alexander the Great to Hitler, have left their mark on us. The tycoon who builds a vast corporate empire, and who amasses more wealth than he can possibly use, does not do so just to get rich. The lust for power, for the excitement of controlling huge enterprises, is in his blood. Even if on a very small scale, the yearning for dominion is in the blood of all of us. It is even in artists and writers, who seek to influence us with their work. Consider the Bible, or the Declaration of Independence, or our revered Constitution, and how they have influenced history. What writer wouldn't like to have that kind of dominion?

Imagine a well-to-do, successful man who has raised a fine family. His physical needs have obviously been met, and he has done his part to ensure the continuation of the species. So he decides to run for president. What motivates him to do that? Curiosity? Love? A passion for dominion? All three? We probably won't be sure until he's president.

SOCIOLOGICAL NOTE

Sex and violence are as American as pepperoni pizza.

HISTORICAL NOTE

"Security" has replaced liberty as the American watchword.

AWARDS

Sports can be competitive because athletic performances can be quantified: speeds and distances can be measured, goals can be counted. But how can we score artistic creations like painting and poetry?

Was Eugene O'Neill a better playwright than Tennessee Williams? Was Picasso a better painter than VanGogh, or Brueghel a better painter than Rembrandt? Was Walt Whitman a better poet than Shelley, or T.S. Eliot a better poet than Archibald MacLeish? How do you pick a champion poet? What do you go by? What would decide whether you gave the blue ribbon to Anne Sexton, Margaret Widdemer, or Edna Millay?

Well, we do have poetry contests, and prizes for poets are awarded, I suppose, by judges who have found a way to measure the immeasurable. I hope this helps, but what really counts is to have people enjoy what you write.

RUNNING AWAY

What kind of a guy would leave his home and his cats and run away with a glamorous lady in a big white Buick to a motel all of ten miles away? A guy like me with a lady like Felicia, that's who — even though the Buick wasn't too white. (Well, we did pause to get it bathed at the Robo-Wash so we could approach Laramie's most elegant motel unsullied by Colorado slush.)

For eighteen enchanted hours I didn't have to drive a car, climb stairs, or walk on rough ground. What's the big deal about that? Try being old, and arthritic, and living on a horse ranch in Howell, and you'll see. Ah, but we feasted deliciously on things we shouldn't eat, and let someone else do the dishes; and we watched "Star Trek" on a channel we don't get in Howell, and drifted off to dreamland in a whole double bed apiece. Next morning was bright and sunny with a hint of spring in the air.

Heading up the highway towards Howell, we found we were as excited about getting home as if we'd been away for a month.

Tell me honestly, now: If you had had your carpet steam cleaned, and were banished form your favorite part of the house, wouldn't you run away too?

O.K., Scotty. Two to beam up.

THOUGHTS

We punish a criminal by cooping him up in a place where he doesn't want to be and having him do things he doesn't want to do. Isn't this what we do when we conscript our young people for wars which they believe are wrong, or when we send our children to school?

THE SPIRIT OF 76

We are beginning to assign roles to our senior citizens the way we used to assign them to women (until the ladies got smart and rebelled). We have organizations, magazines, and even TV programs oriented to senior citizen interests, but I don't have senior citizen interests. I have the same interests I always did. (But I do like those discounts!)

FRATERNAL NOTE

I could join an organization of war veterans or one of retired teachers, since I happen to be both, but I don't see much point to such groups when all their members have in common is something they don't do anymore.

"A THOUSAND POINTS OF LIGHT"

There is nothing ludicrous about this poetic expression. What we make fun of is a politician trying to talk like a poet.

FISCAL NOTE

The millionaire does not offend us because he has a million dollars, but because we don't.

THE BLOODS AND THE CRIPS

There is consternation in the high country these days, because teen-age gangs, like those which have long plagued Los Angeles, have begun to surface in Denver. The tragedy of these young people is that they are superfluous. They are not needed. They have no meaningful role in the dominant society, so they create societies of their own, complete with claims to territory and wars with their rivals. Unfortunately, they engage in criminal activities, from shoplifting to dope peddling, from mugging to murder.

What can we do with these kids? It's not much of a problem in a totalitarian society. Nazi Germany had its Hitler Youth, Communist Russia has its Komsomols and Pioneers. What do we have? The Boy Scouts? I don't think their woodcraft and Indian lore would be too relevant in the inner city; to the Bloods or the Crips they would seem like kid stuff. Put them in the Army? Today's technologically sophisticated armed services don't want cannon fodder. They want men and women of the highest caliber, not delinquents and troublemakers. Appeal to their patriotism? What loyalty do we expect them to feel to a country that has no use for them?

Compulsory school attendance laws, child labor laws, minimum wage laws: all are well-meaning statutes—and all of them help to keep these young people out of the work force and, consequently, out of the American mainstream, leaving them nothing worthwhile to do.

As a member of the Bloods or the Crips a kid counts for something. How can we get him to feel that he doesn't need to be a young criminal to count for something; that as an American, a member of *our* society, he counts for something and he is *not* superfluous?

PATRIOTIC NOTE

Burning an American flag is a tasteless sort of protest and a dumb thing to do, but it does nobody any more harm than burning a dish towel would do. It was a victory for common sense when the Supreme Court ruled that we cannot treat an otherwise harmless gesture as a crime just because it offends us.

Our country is full of people who want to pass laws against what they don't like, but if they all had their way it would no longer be a free country.

HOW TO FEED A HUSBAND

Fry it in butter, serve it with mayonnaise, or put cheese on it, and he will eat it.

—Felicia

ARCHAEOLOGICAL NOTE

Egypt's Great Pyramid is still a wonder of the world, but how much future can there have been for a civilization that would put so much of its resources and energy into this preposterous mausoleum? And was the decline of the Mayas such a mystery, or were they just another culture that collapsed under the burden of its own monuments?

ECONOMIC NOTE

We can soak the rich until they aren't rich anymore. Then who do we soak?

FREEDOM FIGHTERS

We didn't need the Civil War to end slavery, which was on the way out and would have ended soon enough anyway, even though it was sanctioned by the Constitution and, in owning slaves, the Southerners were doing nothing illegal. Anti-slavery sentiment was not confined to the North; the South had abolitionists too, but the Southerners felt that this was their problem and they were the ones to cope with it. They couldn't see letting rabble-rousers like Garrison, or crackpots like John Brown tell them what to do. They had their reasons, both economic and cultural, for wanting independence, but perpetuating slavery wasn't one of them; in fact, the Confederate Constitution outlawed the slave trade. What the Southerners fought for was what we fought for in the Revolution: the right to run their own show.

A BELEAGUERED MINORITY

White South Africans have been in their country as long as we have been in ours, and they have not treated the native African population any worse than we have treated the Indians. The big difference between our countries is that in ours, the white population vastly outnumbers the natives; in South Africa the opposite is true. Before we try to tell the Afrikaners how to run their country, we should bear that in mind. Their elaborate system of racial segregation is too complicated, clumsy, and unfair to be practical in a modern nation, and they are beginning to realize that; but they will have to solve their own problems. Our meddling won't help. South Africa is not South Carolina.

MAKE WAR, NOT LOVE

We can't outlaw tobacco because its production and distribution are a legal industry and an important source of tax revenue; so we go after the users. The anti-smoking campaign is directed, not against tobacco, but against smokers; and it is succeeding. The consumption of cigarettes has been significantly reduced; the rights of non-smokers to clean air are being recognized, and the tobacco companies are hurting.

We tried once to outlaw alcoholic beverages in this country, and Prohibition was a disastrous failure. Now, however, our efforts to curb the abuse of alcohol, such as the campaign against drunk drivers, are succeeding because here, too, we are concentrating on the consumers.

How can we get America off drugs? Maybe we should start with asking: How did America get *on* drugs? Who is buying this junk, and why? And where do they get the staggering sums of money they spend on it? If we want the "war on drugs" to succeed, it will have to become a war on the people who use them. Since their use is so widespread, this would be virtually tantamount to a war on the American people.

That might do more damage than the drugs do.

A HUNDRED PORTRAITS

"Library," said the sweet voice on the telephone. "Can I help you?"

"I hope so," I replied. "The Post Office just sold me a hundred portraits of Grenville Clark, but nobody seems to know who he was."

"Just a minute," the sweet voice answered, and in just a minute I knew all about the man on the 39C stamp.

Grenville Clark was a New York lawyer and co-author of *World Peace through World Law*, an influential book at the time. He was also a power in United World Federalists, one of the world government movements that flourished for a few years after World War II. The world government people held that it is sovereign nations that fight wars, and if the nations of the world could be persuaded to give up their sovereignty, they would give up war along with it. With one government for everybody, the world would be all one country, a kind of United States of Earth, so there would be no reason for war.

Would it work? Alas, I don't think so. For one thing, the principle of national sovereignty is too well entrenched to be willingly abandoned in the foreseeable future. For another, G.K. Chesterton once said that, if you want a United States of Europe, you had better count on a Civil War of Europe. Being all one country didn't prevent our own Civil War, or the one that brought Franco to power in Spain. There would always be a Biafra or a Katanga, a Bangladesh or a Confederate States, struggling for independence; or a country wanting out, as Ireland and South Africa wanted out of the British Commonwealth.

I don't think the principle of national sovereignty in itself is at fault, but rather the scale on which we have allowed it to operate. Luxembourg, Liechtenstein, Switzerland, Costa Rica, Barbados, and Nauru are independent, sovereign nations, but none of them threatens the survival of the species, or the tranquillity of the planet. It is world powers that wage world wars, and maybe it's time we asked if that's all they're good for. It is the superpowers that menace us with hydrogen bombs and "Star Wars" weaponry, not Uruguay and St. Lucia.

If the Confederate States had won their independence, and Deseret, California, Hawaii, and Texas were still independent, and the multitudinous Soviet Republics were really countries of their own, the world just might be a safer place for our kids to grow up in.

NO NUKES = NO WAR?

There are all kinds of warfare going on all over the world all the time, and none of it is being fought with nuclear weapons. If disarmament is the way to end war, then maybe we should concentrate on the kind of hardware that everybody is actually using. One thing to be said for the "balance of terror" created by nuclear weapons is that it does seem to work; at least World War III hasn't started yet.

TREADMILL MUSINGS

A woman's place is where she wants to be.

If people of different races want to live together, they should be able to; the more interracial harmony the better, but people who don't want to live together shouldn't have to.

Since we are a democracy, and we still have the vote, why are we so dissatisfied with our government? I think it is because we do not control the political process that determines who we may vote for.

"It matters not if you win or lose; it's how you play the game." Try and tell that to a Bronco fan.

That a thing is hard to do is not a sufficient reason for doing it. A performance is not necessarily interesting merely because it is difficult.

Since it is human activities that jeopardize the environment, the problem seems to be that there are too many of us. Our first concern should be to get our population explosion under control.

Except for our endless wars, human destructiveness can't compare with the forces of Nature herself, such as floods, droughts, hurricanes, tornados, volcanic eruptions, earthquakes, lightning, hail, forest fires, and whatever cataclysm wiped out the dinosaurs.

Medical science is being used more and more to thwart evolution and assure the survival of the least fit. Keeping alive people who would be better off dead does not strike me as a very humane development. In the natural world, of which we claim to be a part, the fact that the fittest survive means that the unfit do not.

The freedom to succeed is also the freedom to fail.

All life seeks to reproduce itself, and all life lives off other life.

While the fittest members of a species may be the ones to survive, nature has not decided which *species* is the fittest to survive, since we still have a bewildering variety of life forms, from viruses to elephants. Evolution has produced some curious borderline cases. We have fish that go on the land and mammals that live in the sea. We have mammals that lay eggs and fish that don't. We have mammals that fly and birds that don't. Nature, it seems, will try anything, and has yet to make up its mind.

PRO-CHOICE *IS* PRO-LIFE

Does the census count a pregnant woman as two people?

Does your driver's license show the date on which you were conceived?

Do we hold funeral services for a miscarriage?

It would seem to me that a mere fetus, in its early stages, is not a human being with Constitutional Rights any more than an egg is a chicken. I really can't see why it should have any more rights than a tumor. The "rights of the unborn" strikes me as a sentimental delusion. *People* have rights. The unborn are not people.

If a woman wants an abortion, for whatever reason, that is nobody's affair but her own. To make a political issue out of this purely personal matter is preposterous.

BUY AMERICAN

I drive a 1980 Japanese car because nobody in this country made the kind of car that I wanted at a price I could afford at that time. Buy American? Of course. I bought my car from an American dealer right here in Wyoming. It burns American gasoline, it is serviced by American mechanics, and I pay *very* American taxes on it. My little Subaru, it seems, is helping to provide jobs for quite a few of my fellow Americans.

SECURITY

I'm all for protecting our country, but not for the way we've been doing it. We continue stockpiling weapons that cannot be used without destroying civilization, and I don't see much protection in that. Our policy of meddling in the affairs of other countries, and trying to run the whole world, antagonizes just about everybody, and I don't see much protection in that either.

WISDOM

"Anything worth doing is worth doing well." Taken too seriously, this wise old saying can lead to a picayune perfectionism in petty pursuits, more frustrating than fruitful. Moderation and common sense will tell us that much of what we do does not need to be done extremely well, it just needs to be done.

POLITICAL NOTE

Liberals are people who want the government to take care of everybody at my expense.

EXEGETICAL NOTE

Because of the Bible's religious origins, we tend to think that only religious people read it. This is too bad, because you don't need to be religious to enjoy this marvelous collection of ancient history, philosophy, poetry, folklore, and stories. Because of our Constitutional ban on religion in the schools, our young people are growing up unacquainted with one of the great treasures of our cultural heritage.

ETHNIC NOTE

It is not unreasonable to suppose that people, radically different from us in appearance, might be different from us in other ways too. It is when we claim that one race is superior to another that we get in trouble. I might be superior to an African pygmy in Howell, Wyoming, but which of us would be the better man in the equatorial rain forest?

ZOOLOGICAL NOTE

We cannot judge a gorilla by how good a nuclear physicist he would make. We have to judge him by how good a gorilla he makes.

MY SMALL AND GENTLE ONES

Cats Magazine devotes a section to cat stories by its readers. I submitted this true story about my first cat, and it was published in the issue of March, 1987.

THE WILDLIFE CONNECTION

Once upon a time, back in New England, I shared a first floor apartment with a little calico cat named Peppy. Peppy had the run of the apartment, the basement, and the back yard at all time. So, apparently, did some of the local wild-life.

My bedroom adjoined the kitchen, and one night I was awakened by a scuffling noise in the vicinity of Peppy's dinner dish. I turned on the light and there, black-and-white, beady-eyed and bushy-tailed, helping himself to Peppy's dinner, was a skunk.

Panic time in suburbia! Where was Peppy? Dogs of all sizes knew her spirited defense of her turf. What would she do about a skunk in the house? I was imagining having to evacuate our happy home, and of my upstairs tenants having to evacuate their happy home, when Peppy emerged from a patrol of the living room, moseyed over to the skunk, and demurely sat down beside him while he finished her dinner.

This guy was her guest.

Dinner over, Peppy and her handsome friend trotted side by side down the basement stairs and out into the night. Next morning there was not the faintest whiff to suggest that a skunk had come to dinner, and I began to wonder if I hadn't dreamed the whole episode. Peppy was curled up beside me, nonchalantly purring in my ear, but something about the look on her face told me that it had all really happened.

SO MANY PUSSIES

Let's hear what the pussies are telling me of:
Poki wants breakfast and Tommy wants love,
Little black Bonnie wants petting and talk,
Polly and Shiner want to go for a walk,
While faithful old Fluffy wants a warm spot to dream
Of summertime hunting down by the stream.
With so many pussies, I always know
That I'll be meowed to wherever I go!

A THOUGHT

I tied a shiny ball on the end of a string for my cat to play with, only to find that what she really wanted to chase was the string. The game would be no fun if she couldn't catch it once in a while, even if she didn't know what to do with it after she caught it — except to let it go so she could chase it again. Is here a moral for us in here somewhere?

SYMBIOSIS

My Poki curls beneath my light
As if she had a perfect right
To settle down there for the night.
She hasn't felt a need to ask
If this is where a cat may bask.
I want to work right where I found her
But I guess I'll have to work around her—
Reasoning doesn't work with her:
I've tried, but all she does is purr.
In fourteen years of nights and days,
It seems we've learned each other's ways:
Where Poki settles, Poki stays.

PASTURE-WALKING

Our garage is home to Mabel, Sabrina, Trixie, Gray Brother, Little One, Polly, and Shiner. The first three are vehicles. The last four are cats. Big, gentle, three-legged Gray Brother is still the fastest cat in the West. Black Little One is our feisty Halloween cat. Sweet little tiger-striped Polly stands on my feet and squeaks 'till I pet her. Her big brother Shiner is our Kliban-type cat, and he never says anything.

    I emerge from the garage to find four little faces looking up at me expectantly, and I see disappointment in four pairs of eyes as I whiz away on my bike. I come back with the mail and take off again, this time on my Honda four-wheeler (that one's Trixie) for some other mission. More disappointment. Finally I put Trixie away and appear with my old silver cane and start walking. Four furry faces light up, for this is what they've been waiting for. As I amble here and there in the front pasture, I am accompanied by four happy cats.

They dash off to chase a grasshopper here, check out a gopher hole there, nibble a little grass, sniff a cactus blossom, or chase and roughhouse with each other, returning from time to time for a rub behind the ears or a little feline-to-human conversation. Wherever I go, they are not far away, and when I come home, they come with me.

I do not call them. They are not trained to follow me around, but whenever I am out walking, at least one or two, sooner or later appear beside me. I was wondering aloud one day to our daughter Summer, "Why do such notoriously independent creatures as cats do anything like this."

"They know you love them," she said.

FOR POKI

She met me at my study door
And rode upon my shoulder
And helped me with my desk work
And curled up purring in my lap
During "Prairie Home Companion,"
But love can't keep a cat alive
Forever, though we shared some years
Beyond what's normal for a cat,
And still she tried with all her love
To go on being Poki. Now I must give
Another little cat
A home and love, and I must try
To go on being me.

CAT SONG

Bonnie and Tommy both love me —
They have assured me of that —
But little calico Maddie
Is my personal library cat.
When I go for a walk in the pasture
Bonnie and Tommy like to come too,
But little calico Maddie
Is here for me when we get through.
Bonnie and Tommy rub noses;
They're very good friends, you see,
But little calico Maddie
Is the cat who rubs noses with me.

FEBRUARY THAW

Bonnie and Tommy and I —
Two everyday cats
And an old poet —
Have been out walking
On a summer island
In a winter sea.
This kindly sky,
This gentle air,
This warming sun
Call for sparkling waters,
Not ice still white and solid
On our river, large
Exotic blossoms flaming
On big trees, not naked
Twigs on our little aspen,

Lush fruits and lawns,
Not brown dry grass
And shriveled weeds;
But strolling in
This winter scene
With summer weather,
The cats and I
Can dream of when
It's really summer.

FIRST WALK

Old joints pain me when it's cold
But today I'm feeling bold
Because it's springtime! (So I'm told.)

Pussycats! Come walk with me.
Let's go see what we can see
And talk to that birdie in our tree.

We'll stroll the pasture, and once more
We'll find some features to explore
(Although we've seen them all before.)

I will walk, but you may run
Where the greening's just begun
Under the equinoctial sun.

THE LANGUAGE WE SPEAK

HOW CLOSE DO WE COME?

Here's an interesting intellectual experience: Take a book you are familiar with, and read it in another language. The Bible is a good book for this, since it is readily available in hundreds of different tongues. Presumably it says the same things in Yiddish, French, or Hawaiian that it does in English, Georgian, or Greek, but are they *really* the same? How close actually are they?

When we translate, we must translate not only the words, but the grammar, and not only those two things, but the culture as well. This is why no two translations are exact, one-to-one equivalents. At best they say *approximately* the same things.

STYLISTIC NOTE

We may have unduly maligned the cliche, since most of what we say has to be cliche if people are to understand us. We are baffled by the work of artists and writers who try to be too original, because they have failed to express themselves in a language we know.

TRANSFORMATIONAL GRAMMAR

Transformational grammar began with the idea that the structure of any grammatical sentence in a given language can be produced, or generated, by modifying or elaborating the structure of one of a small number of basic sentence types. The latter were called "kernel" sentences, and variations of them produced by a set of ordered rules were called "transforms" of them.

Modern transformational-generative (TG) grammar has gotten much more sophisticated and complex than that. The "surface structure" of what we actually say is arrived at by transformational processes from a hypothetical underlying, or "deep," structure. Since the latter is not accessible for study, there has been some controversy over the question of what it consists of.

Structural, or descriptive, grammar examines a sample of a language sufficiently large to draw some general conclusions about it. TG grammar, on the other hand, purports to offer a means of generating new grammatical sentences rather than merely analyzing sentences that have already been spoken or written. The transformationalists, then, have tried to give us a sentence-making grammar, instead of a sentence-describing one. Have they succeeded?

A sentence-making grammar should be able to say what its raw material is; what are its sentences generated *from*? The elusive and controversial "deep structure" does not appeal to me as a satisfactory answer.

Musical notes can be generated electronically, and I am sure that a computer could be programmed to generate Beethoven's 5th Symphony—but what would such a program tell us about how an orchestra does it? The transformational grammarians give us rules for generating sentences, but is this the way *people* generate them? Do we really go through all those phrase-structure rules, transformational rules, morphophonemic rules, raising rules, deletion rules, flip-flop rules, etcetera,[1] when we talk to each other?

The transformationalists remind me of the old-fashioned prescriptive grammarians, with their fondness for making up rules instead of trying to find out what's really going on. TG grammar is an intriguing contribution to linguistic theory, but what is it telling us about how real languages actually work?[2]

---

[1] See *English and English Linguistics* by Randal L. Whitman (Holt, Rinehart & Winston, New York 1975); and *Modern Linguistics, the Results of Chomsky's Revolution*, by Neil Smith and Deirdre Wilson (Indiana University Press, Bloomington, 1979).

[2] It is only fair to point out that transformationalism is the mainstream of current linguistic thought, and mine is a minority view. For more prestigious swimmers against the current, see Charles F. Hockett's *The State of the Art* (Mouton & Co., The Hague, 1968) and Ian Robinson's *The New Grammarians' Funeral* (Cambridge University Press, New York, 1975).

WHAT IS A LANGUAGE?

I said in one of my essays[1]: "The English language, then, is not what any one person actually says, but the *system* according to which he constructs what he says...Looked upon, not as the actual operations of speakers, but as the system according to which the operations that constitute speech are performed; the concept of a language is seen to be something of an abstraction."

The transformational grammarians offer us a set of rules for operating the system, but my feeling is that their rules are constructs of the grammarians rather than a model of what actually takes place when people talk to each other. I furthermore feel that transformational grammar, despite it theoretical interest, is too complicated and cumbersome to be of any practical use.

My definition of a language was all right as far as it went, but language is a human activity, something people *do*, and not just their method of doing it. There is a French language because people speak French.

It is our command of a language's system that enables us to understand sentences that have not been uttered before, so long as they conform to the system and contain words that we know.

---

[1] "Phonemes of What?", in *Before the Wind*

"IN...OF" VS. "IN THE...OF"

If you returned from a camping trip and told me that you had slept "in the back of the truck," I would understand this to mean that you had bedded down *in* this vehicle; but if you reported that you had slept "in back of the truck," I would understand you to mean that you had unrolled your sleeping bag on the ground behind it.

If you wanted to know where an artist's studio was, and I told you that it was "in back of his house," you would look for a separate structure behind the dwelling; but if I had said it was "in the back of his house," you would assume it to be in the rear part of the dwelling itself.

If a doctor's office is "in front of his house," it's in a building of its own and the house is behind it; but if it's "in the front of the house," it occupies the front part of the dwelling itself.

In "in the front of" or "in the back of," the definite article clearly marks "front" and "back" as nouns designating the forward or rearward part of something; but if we leave out the article and say "in back of," then what part of speech is "back"? It would seem that the meaning of "in back of" is not just the sum of its parts; the expression is rather a kind of idiom meaning "behind," and perhaps should be written as one word, the way we do with "nevertheless." The same goes for "in front of" (though, unlike "behind," "before," as a one-word synonym, is distinctly archaic).[1]

Does the definite article always make a difference in expressions like these? Well, we never say "in the spite of," and whether we say "in place of" or "in the place of" doesn't seem to make any real difference. There is, however, a difference between "in the case of" and "in case of." The latter means "in the event of" some occurrence, whereas the former refers to an instance or situation under discussion. "In case of the Falkland Islands, the Argentine claim seems rather thin" doesn't sound quite right. To fix it, we put in the article and make it, "In the case of..." On the other hand, "In the case of fire, call 911," while intelligible, would sound more natural with the "the" left out.

Note that it is not whether we use a definite or an indefinite article that makes the difference between "in the back of," and "in back of," or "in the case of" and "in case of." The difference results from either using or omitting just the definite article.

Pointing all this out, alas, does not clarify any general rule of English grammar, but merely notes a very few special cases. Confronted with phenomena of this kind, foreigners learning our language may well wonder if it consists of anything *but* special cases!

[1] Nowadays "before" normally situates its object in time rather than space.

"MUCH," "VERY," AND "VERY MUCH"

"MUCH"

Not long ago I heard that the expression "not much good" is "wrong," though I couldn't see why, since I have heard it used by all the "best" people. Its meaning is perfectly clear to anybody who hears it, and I have never known it to offend anyone's taste. The difficulty seems to be in the rather odd and special ways that we use the little word "much."

For one thing, "much" is used as an intensifier with the comparative degree of adjectives, but not with the other degrees. We say:

| much better | much more beautiful | much more |
| much bigger | much more interesting | much looser |

But we don't say:
| *much good | *much beautiful | *much much |
| *much big | *much interesting | *much loose |

Nor do we say:
| *much best | *much most beautiful | *much most |
| *much biggest | *much most interesting | *much loosest |

Aha! I've just said myself that we don't say "much good." No, we don't—*when "good" is an adjective*. But it can also be used as a noun:
Much good may it do!
We aren't doing much good here.
Much good is done by our missionaries.

"Much," in these cases, is not an intensifier, but a kind of indefinite quantifier meaning "a lot of," as in the following:
Too much candy is bad for you.
There isn't much more.
We haven't spent much money.

"Much" itself is sometimes a noun:
Don't eat much of that.
They really don't have much.
He never was good for much.

The difference between "not very good" and "not much good" is not one of "correct" versus "incorrect" usage, but is both a semantic and grammatical one. "Not very good" refers to quality whereas "not much good" refers to usefulness and is equivalent to "not good for much."

    Our plans were not very good

"Good," in this sentence, is obviously a predicate adjective, a subjective complement stating that the quality of the plans was poor (even though they may have been good for a great deal). But what part of speech is "good" in the following sentence?

    Our plans were not much good.

Here "good" is also a subjective complement, but it's not an adjective because, as we have seen, the positive degree of adjectives cannot take "much" as a modifier. "Good," in this case, is therefore a predicate noun, like "help" or "use" in the following sentences, since it has the same sort of meaning:

    Our plans were not much help.
    Our plans were not much use.

(It is interesting that when "much" is used in other ways than as an intensifier for the comparative degree of adjectives, it almost always seems to appear in a negation of some kind. "Not much" seems to be a commoner expression than "much.")

"VERY"

"Very," on the other hand, *can* be used with the positive degree of adjectives but not with the other degrees. We say:

very good	very beautiful	very much
very big	very interesting	very loose

But we don't say:

*very better	*very more beautiful	*very more
*very bigger	*very more interesting	*very looser

What about expressions like these?
That's the very loosest fit I can give you.
That's the very best car you can buy.
I sold him the very biggest one in the store.

This "very" is not the intensifier of "very good," but an adverb meaning "actually," "veritably," or "truly."

"VERY MUCH"

While we can say "much better" but not "*very better," we *can* say "very much better," "very much more beautiful," "very much more," or "very much looser." "Very" can't intensify the comparative degree of adjectives by itself, but it can intensify the intensifier, that is, it can modify "much."

ALL OF WHICH GOES TO SHOW...

The real grammar of English is much more subtle and complex than we native speakers usually realize, which is why foreigners have so much trouble learning our language. As Werner Winter once said in *Language*, "...to account for all that actually occurs in a natural language, we must be content to live with the messiness that goes with it."*

---

* Werner Winter, "Transforms without Kernels?", *Language*, Vol. 41, No. 3 part 1, July-September 1965.

DOES ENGLISH HAVE AN ETHICAL DATIVE?

Well, maybe not a real one, but certain prepositional phrases introduced by "on" do somewhat resemble one; for example:

> He might have gotten away with it if his sister hadn't told their mother *on him*.
> They had complete faith in that bank until it went belly-up *on them*.
> The motor died *on me* just as I turned into the driveway.
> As soon as you know the game, they change the rules *on you*.
> Felicia planted two rows of carrots and the rabbits ate up every last one of them *on her*.

The "on..." phrase is a gratuitous insertion. It is not essential to the sentence. The meaning would be just as clear if *on him*, *on me*, etc. were left out, yet these expressions are common in everyday conversational English — so what are they for? I think they emphasize the fact that the event described affected someone personally; it was more than just something in the news. All of us are sometimes adversely affected by actions that don't actually do anything to us. In each of the sample sentences above this is the case, and I think the "on..." phrases emphasize this fact.

The bank didn't do anything to those who had faith in it, but what it did certainly affected them. The rabbits did not attack Felicia, but what they did attack certainly affected her. It is plain from the "on her" phrase that she did not plant the carrots for the benefit of the rabbits.

These sentences, on the other hand, are not examples of the phenomenon:

> He was standing under the ladder when a bucket of paint fell *on him*.
> The shopping cart rolled over *on her*.

These sentences refer to things that directly happened to the victim rather than events that merely affected him/her in some roundabout way. Note that in these cases, the "on..." phrase is not superfluous. Without *on him*, we would not know where the bucket of paint ended up, and without *on her*, we would not know of her involvement in the accident. Thus, not every prepositional phrase introduced by "on" is an ethical dative; but it may well be one if, as we saw above, it is tacked onto the sentence and is not necessary to it.

The "for..." phrase in the following conversation may also be regarded as a kind of ethical dative:

It snowed on Mother's Day this year, but Valentine's Day was like spring.

Well, that's Wyoming *for you*.

NEW SUFFIXES

Languages grow and change over the years, and Chaucer's English is not the English we speak today. Even the English spoken by the Pilgrims at Plymouth would sound strange to our ears. American and British English have become so different that H.L. Mencken called his monumental work on our version *The American Language*.

Various forces at work, both within and upon a language, cause it to change in the course of time. One of the most potent such forces, and one that's still at work, is analogical extension; the creation of new forms, or of new usages for existing ones, on the model of ones we already have. Among its more colorful products are some special-purpose new suffixes.

—ATHON. This is used for any nonstop special-purpose activity, on the analogy of "marathon." We have "telethon" for a nonstop television show to raise money for charity, and a local car dealer has even advertised a "Toyotathon" to sell his product.

—ARAMA. This one, derived from "panorama," has been around for a long time to designate any large-scale presentation. "Cinerama" was a kind of wide-screen super movie. A local horse club has put on a kind of fair they called a "horse-a-rama."

—AHOLIC, spun off from "alcoholic" to denote any kind of overindulgence. "Workaholics" are people who get too wrapped up in their work, and "saltaholics" use too much salt.

—GATE. This one is my favorite. It is, of course, derived from the Watergate scandal that brought down the Nixon administration. It has been extended to cover any scandal involving government officials. We have had "Iran-gate" and now even "S&L-gate."

—ABLE. As new applications for a time-honored, respectable suffix, how about "flushable" and "microwaveable"?

(For more on analogical extension, see page 24 of 7000 Feet Closer to Heaven.)

AN 'AGENTIVE-POSSESSIVE'?

The possessive case of proper names or personal pronouns in English does not always indicate a possessor of something, but sometimes the *doer* or something.

(1) I dropped an egg on Donna's clean floor. [Donna is our cleaning lady. She does not own the floor, we do; but Donna cleaned it.]

(2) Dr. Miller is an artist in his spare time. I really like his pictures. ["His pictures" does not refer to a private art gallery owned by the doctor, but to pictures painted by him.]

(3) Everybody likes Gil's soap. [The soap is not a possession that people admire, but something that Gil makes.]

(4) Summer's massage relieved my back pain. [The massage is something Summer *does*, rather than something she has.]

The agentive-possessive can be used in a passive sense, too; that is, it can indicate the undergoer, rather that the performer, of an action:

(5) We saw Summer's picture in the paper. [This could conceivably be a picture owned or made by Summer, but, in this case, it was a picture taken by a news photographer.]

(6) David showed us his bruises. [David does possess the bruises in a sense, and he may even be said to have made them by something he did, but they are the result of an accident, an experience undergone by David.]

(7) We were impressed by their ratings. [The ratings were not something they owned or did, but were conferred upon them by others.]

DOMESTIC VERSES

THE MACINTOSH BLUES

She put garbage in, got garbage back
Until she was ready to blow her stack:
"You're not being user-friendly, Mac!"
For she had wrestled with MacWrite
Until she suffered from mouse-byte.
(Note that I spelled that with a "y",
The reason being, of course, that I
Realize it's an important matter
From a computer freak to know the patter.)
Then said she, "Now listen, Mac!
I think that I will bite you back!"
Now upon the glowing screen
In fancy type these words were seen:
"Do that, and you will run the risk
That you will overload the disk."
At this point, then, the lady said,
"I should have done MacPaint instead;
Because the virtue of MacPaint
Is it makes you an artist when you ain't;
But now it's time for me to head
For my little old MacBed."

FURZLE-BUSHES

"Come with me, and I will show
Where the furzle-bushes grow
And push the fence posts to and fro.
Chickadiddles roost here too,
So here is what I'd have you do:
I'd have you hack them down and chop them,
Bushwhack them and lop them
Right down to the roots thereof."
So admonished me my love
As cheerily she urged me, "Go!"
But when I went, old bones said, "Whoa!"
And the vertebrae said "No!"
(Furzle-bushes are pretty tough
And it wasn't long 'till I had enough.)
Alas! I may have been ambitious
But I couldn't fulfill my true love's wishes,
So I had to go back to washing dishes.
This tale should have a point behind it,
And if it does, I hope you find it.

DUMPSTER SONG

We would stash the stuff and hide it
When we could no more abide it.
But to make the piles go down
We had to truck the stuff to town,
Which wasn't too much fun
For whoever made the run.

(I'm just a lowly dumpster
But I stand here proud and tall
As you listen for the rumble
And prepare your stuff to haul,
So get your act together,
For I will make it plain,
The dumpster man must never
Have to make this trip in vain.)

We have our river and our land,
We have a house that's pretty grand,
But what I want to show to you
Is a feature that is new:
A collector for our trash
That no longer must we stash.

(Hear the rumble, heed the call,
Winter, springtime, summer, fall,
The dumpster man will get it all.)

FANTASY

One of them brought me exotic tea
And one of them brought me beer;
Another brought me just herself,
Brimming with love and cheer.

Now if I were a god and not just me,
How would I choose among these three?
Which of them would my dearest be?

SECURITY

The dumpster man was here today.
I thought he might take me away
But he always lets me stay:
My true love keeps him at bay.

The stars are bright, the sky is clear,
But a bitter wind is blowing here,
Yet winter's chill I need not fear
Because I know my love is near.

I think it's what the Lord intends
And this the message that he sends:
Her healing influence extends
To distant daughters, many friends.

For horses, pussycats, and me
And even for our smallest tree
Our world's secure as it can be
Because my love is here, you see.

She's luscious and lovely besides all this.
I think I'll give my love a kiss.

A VALENTINE

However dim the winter's light,
However dark the winter night,
I know that you will make it bright—
   So now it's time for me to say,
"Be my Valentine today."
(Since you're my true love anyway.)

VALENTINE SONG

Were I to give you all my love,
Would I then run out,
So all our kids and kittycats
Would have to do without?
Anyway, I think I'll try;
It seems to be a lover's lot
To have what he can't quantify—
The more he gives, the more he's got.

JANUARY SONG

On the thirteenth day of Christmas
My true love said to me,
"The grass is green in Seattle,
Oh, this is the place to be."

I looked out my kitchen window
And all I could see was snow,
But we were at ease
At twenty degrees
(Though the windchill was twenty below.)

Yes, I wasn't too unhappy
To view the arctic scene
Because I knew my true love
Was where the grass was green.

19th ANNIVERSARY

10 and 20 are nice round
Statistical-type numbers
Dear to actuaries
And people who celebrate things
(They like the zeros in them);
But we've been married
19 years, and 19's a prime
Number so it must be that
My years with you have been
Nothing less than
PRIME TIME!

BEING

a higher art than doing
is perhaps to be
as when my love and I
at the kitchen table
being together
just watch it rain

ANNIVERSARY

How long's a year? It all depends
On who you're married to:
Some twenty-three of mine went by
Like they were only two —
And all the ones that passed so fast
Were the years I've spent with you.

TREADMILL

she steps out briskly
for her walk
while motionless beside her
I relax
yet have no trouble
keeping up
and so my love and I
each at our own pace
can be together
going nowhere
isn't technology
wonderful

PRESENCE

I may not catch a sight of you
Or hear a single sound,
But I can sense your presence
And feel that you're around.
"Absence makes the heart grow fonder." —
I know that's very true,
But here's a fact to ponder:
Your presence does that too.

24th ANNIVERSARY

(We were married on April 22)

This day on which we made our vow
To cherish one another:
Did we realize how
Great a day it really was?
They call it Earth Day now!

Our twenty-fourth? What can I do
But count by dozens my years with you?
Even so, they're far too few.

SPOUSE

In a quarter century I have found,
My true love makes the world go round.

Kids and cats and horses thrive,
And I am very much alive.

The home fires burn, the water flows,
Thanks to what my true love knows.

She gives me love and care and cheer.
She makes Christmas last all year.

BIRD SONG

The lordly goose, the gentle dove
Once in a lifetime fall in love.

The message these birds have for us:
We too should be monogamous.

Notwithstanding birds or men,
I think I'll fall in love again.

I will fall in love anyway—
With my own sweetheart every day.

25th ANNIVERSARY

Twenty-five's the magic number
Of the years I've spent with you,
And custom says we honor it
With a Maundy Thursday do,
Since one and two and twenty-two
And seventeen and in between
Were magic too.

EQUINOX

Your birthday is a special thing:
The first green shows, the bluebirds sing;
Every year it brings the spring.

The calendar's not really true —
(It doesn't know what birthdays do.)
It's not the equinox, it's you.

SILVER WEDDING

I would like the world to see
What my true love gave to me,
But it can't be hung upon the wall
Or be, in fact, displayed at all.
What was this present
From my wife?
Just the best quarter century
Of my life!

A VALENTINE FOR FELICIA

Here's my favorite mystery:
How can you so wondrous be
After so many years with me?

Ever delightful, always new,
But best of all, you're always you.

"We do not celebrate this day,"
Is what I think I've heard you say—
But I love you anyway.

SANDY, HOME FOR A VISIT

what shall it be
for this dark lovely daughter
of ancient people
of a harsh land
our daughter too
a pot of tea
is soon empty
but a pot of love
stays full

NEXT VISIT

When they come again
I will be young again.
I will be handsomer
Than my athletic son.
I will skip over the hills
Like a biblical roebuck
And I will rejoice
That these are my daughters.

A DAY IN AUGUST

Today my Lisa's twenty-three.
I wonder how this came to be:
It happened oh so fast, you see.

A horse of course, a pussycat,
A goose, a sheep — some beast like that —
But dollies weren't where it was at.

4-H and school, a wedding too —
Yes, there was always something new —
We never lacked for things to do.

Now beneath another sun
Her new life has just begun
(And we hope she's having fun.)

Today my Lisa's twenty-three
And she's very dear to me!

FOR CAROL AND SUMMER (II)

on their 21st birthday

"You don't even look like girls!"
I can't believe I said that once, but now
You're not babies anymore,
Or even kids; not juvenile headaches
Or even minors, but officially mature!
You can own real estate,
Buy booze, run for office and become
Governor of Florida and deny reprieves
To the likes of Bundy. You're citizens
Of a superpower and can pay for war
With very adult taxes,
Serve on a jury, sue and be sued;
Marry without anyone's consent,
But always you're my daughters
And I love you, and I hope
You'll vote Libertarian
But I'll still love you
If you don't.

NOVEMBER SONG

For my daughters in Florida

How the rheumatism rankles
When the pastures twist my ankles
And the stairs raise havoc with my knee!
Now the weather's getting colder
And I am getting older,
Is this the kind of place where I should be?
Or should it be a condo
Way down in warm Orlando,
In the country of the sunshine and the sea?

Assuming we'd find takers,
Could we ever sell The Acres
And leave the home and people that we know?
(At least we've got Victoria,
Sabrina, Flash and Gloria,
For anytime we get the urge to go.)
But could we trade our lovely mountains
For some southern parks and fountains,
Then find to our surprise we missed the snow?

However much we dearly love you
And are always thinking of you
And how tempted we might be to roam
Where the terrain never freezes
And the gentle tropic breezes
Bring a breath of salty ocean foam,
We probably will stay here,
Live and work and play here;
There's something in our hearts that calls it home.

A BALLAD FOR MAY 23RD

The lawn is green
For the wedding scene,
The judge will be out from town
(And we have Plan B
For where we'll be
In case the rain comes down.)

It's only May
So who can say
What flowers might bloom for Sandy?
But there *must* be flowers
For these joyful hours
So let's keep some bouquets handy.

We see buds on the trees
As they sway in the breeze,
But will they be leafing out for us?
Or must we wait
Till a later date,
When we hear the peepers' chorus?

A Wyoming spring
Can be anything
From daffodils to snow,
But this special day
In the month of May
Shall be just for Sandy and Joe.

TO WYOMING

in her Centennial Year

It's been a quarter-century
Since you called me west
From my green hills
And ocean shores
To teach your sons and daughters
Just for a year; but something in
Your pristine peaks,
Your sparkling streams,
Your crystal air,
Your easy ways
And kindly people
Has made me stay
Until your birthday
Which, as a native son
I cannot honor, but
May I claim at least
I was adopted?

WINTER WALK

Gray clouds against cold sky,
Streaked and flattened
And combed straight
By arctic winds
(Unlike the towering palatial
Clouds of summer sailing
In their warm sea);
Pale sun glinting
On the river's ice,
Shadows lengthening
At three o'clock
As the wind comes up.
The cats who keep me
Company on my walks
Do not appear;
They don't expect me
In the winter.
This ground I've walked
So many years
And known so well
Through all the seasons
Surrounds the home wherein
My true love dwells;
Perhaps that's what is good
About a winter walk.

LILAC TIME

With green below and blue above,
It's lilac time in Howell, love!

I'm sorry if they make you sneeze:
Their fragrance on the summer breeze
Was only meant to lure the bees.

Why can't their purple beauty stay?
"Better a queen for just a day
Than not at all," the wise men say.

I have a queen though I'm no king.
She's my queen in everything
And every season (not just spring.)

Oh, it's green below and blue above,
And oh, it's lilac time, my love!

THE BALLAD OF NUTTER'S LAWN

(Our neighbors gave a lawn-warming party to celebrate their new turf. I wrote this for the occasion.)

Environmentalists would be dismayed
To see the lawn that you have made.
Passing by the other day,
Here is what I heard them say:
"Creating beauty where none was
Is contrary to Nature's laws.
It is our duty to protect
The weeds and sagebrush you reject.
Only the antelope must play;
People should just go away.
We'd bring back tyrannosaurus if we could,
And sabertooth grumbling in the wood."
But we like Suzanne and John;
Won't they please let them stay on?

ALMOST HOME

Big clouds of cotton
From an angel's vitamin bottle
Hang like chandeliers
From a blue ceiling
And trail their see-through skirts
Across the road on which,
Homeward bound from friends up north,
We're in a sudden world
Of mist and snow,
Then up beyond the old hotel
That Wister's Virginian made famous,
We swing south at last
On our own highway
With the UP tracks
Running alongside.
The clouds move on
And so do we, and feel
How good is being
Almost home.

FOR WENDY AND WANDA

en route to horse trials

what can we do
for these young adventurers
but nourish them well
give them a hug
to wish them luck
and for their safety
sneak in a prayer

Our religious denomination has a Service Committee that served as a model for the Peace Corps; helping people to help themselves. During the Christmas season many of us place a small Service Committee collection box on our dinner tables so we may feed it — the guest at our table — when we feed ourselves, in the hope that someone who might otherwise go hungry may get something to eat. Who might that someone be?

A GUEST AT OUR TABLE

Gathered round
Our Christmas table
We did not see her
But we knew
That she was there
And we could tell
That probably
Her skin was dark
And that she spoke
A language that
We did not know.
Somehow we saw
The pleading in
Her haunted eyes
And then we heard
Across the centuries
A gentle voice
That we remembered.
"Welcome her," it told us,
"She is your sister."